Pets Who Want to Kill Themselves

Pets Who Want to Kill Themselves

Duncan Birmingham

THREE RIVERS PRESS

NEW YORK

Published in the United States by Three Rivers Press,
an imprint of the Crown Publishing Group,
a division of Random House, Inc., New York.
www.crownpublishing.com

Three Rivers Press and the Tugboat design
are registered trademarks of Random House, Inc.

Library of Congress Cataloging-in-Publication Data
Birmingham, Duncan.
Pets who want to kill themselves / by Duncan Birmingham.—Ist ed.
I. Pets—Humor. I. Title.
PN623I.P42B57 2009
8I8'.602—dc22   2009022565

ISBN 978-0-307-58988-0

Printed in Singapore

Design by Elizabeth Rendfleisch

IO 9 8 7 6 5 4 3 2 I

First Edition

To all the good-humored pet lovers
who generously submitted
their great photos
despite the really scary title.

"They say the suicide rate skyrockets over Christmas. In my owner's case, I can only hope."

"Can you die of an ice cream headache? God, I hope so."

"A *fake* tie?! How am I supposed to hang myself with this?"

"Forget the ten paces. Just shoot me now."

"Trust me, fellas. Underwater she looks just like Daryl Hannah."

Fluffy read the instructions twice before deciding to classify herself as a "delicate cotton."

"Are you dressing me to look like a power forward or a power bottom?"

"Jeez . . . I only asked for a trim."

"Fetch the paper yourself. I've got eight gold medals, asshole!"

"My safe word is 'Alpo.'"

"Ay carumba! I want to be deported."

"I look like a moron. Why the hell can't I ever be mustard?"

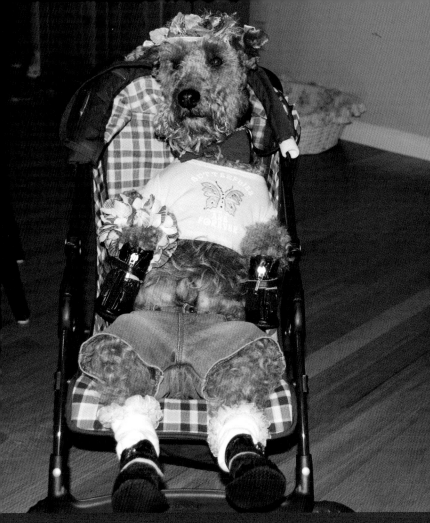

"On second thought, forget the dog park and let's stay in."

Socks had an adorable new game of hiding in frying pans, microwaves, and other dangerous appliances.

"I thought Richard Gere's hamster had it tough."

"My name? My name's whatever you want it to be, baby."

"Didn't Michael Vick go to jail for this kind of thing?"

"You're hilarious, honey. Now boil me already."

Running away from her owner was easy, but Princess realized "blending in" would be a whole other challenge.

"I'd be much cooler with this if we switched outfits."

"There's this great new invention—
it's called a sticker book!"

"I can't wait to lay a steaming hot Easter egg on the new rug."

"Please, just let sleeping dogs die."

"Okay, sweetie, show me on the dog where he touched you."

"There's nothing good on TV.
Whaddya say we marry the cats?"

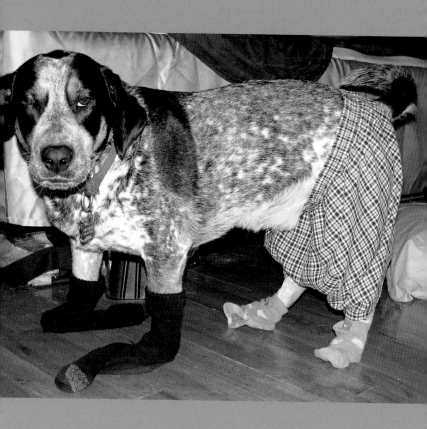

"You could have at least dressed me in *clean* undies."

"*Dry* dog food? Fry me up a porkchop before I bitch-paw you."

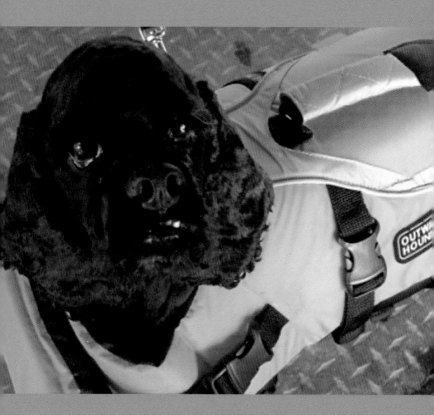

"No offense, skipper, but do you have anything with more of a 'vest filled with heavy rocks' look?"

"I told you, I *am* making a 'funny' face!"

"She dresses me like this 'cause it's cheaper than getting me spayed."

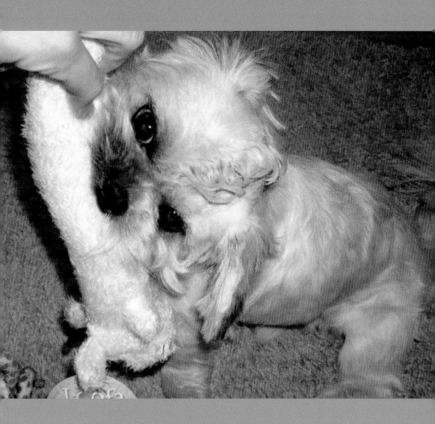

"I hate my haircut. I look like Shrek wiped his ass with my head."

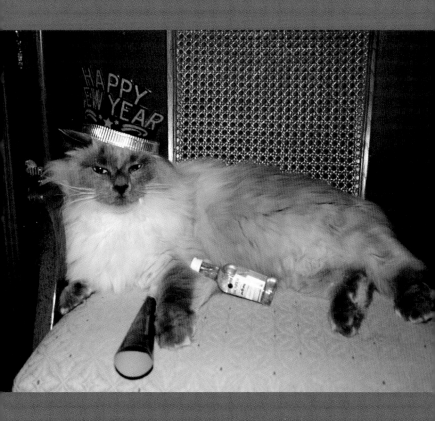

"My New Year's resolution is to not make it to next New Year's."

"I'm 56 in dog years. Is this J-Lo phase ever gonna end?"

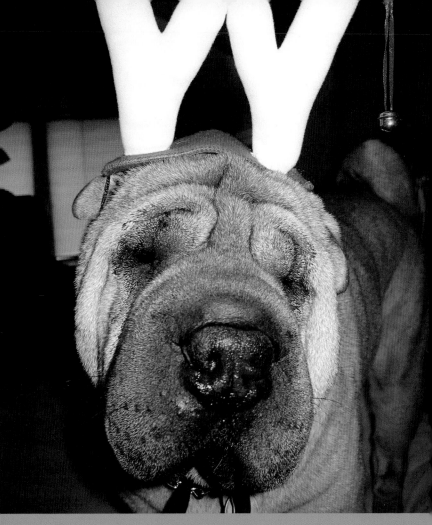

"The cruel irony is the sadder I am,
the more adorable I look."

"Sure they treat you like a king now, but pretty soon you'll be eating table scraps and sleeping in your own poop, too."

"Is this your not-so-subtle way of telling me I stink?"

"C'mon in! I just warmed up the water for you!"

"The cowboy hat's fine; it's the assless chaps I'm not crazy about."

"Are you training me for the Iditarod or just being a colossal prick?"

"Really? Isn't it bad enough you dress yourself like an asshole?"

"Aren't you gonna do something?!
They're spooning on *my* bed!"

"It's better with my hair like this.
Thankfully, I can't see myself-."

"Robin, fetch me the batgun so I can blow out my batbrains."

"Whatever Paula Abdul's smoking, I need some too."

"I wish this costume came with a gun . . . and opposable thumbs."

Rusty finally found a way to combine his two greatest passions: double-fudge ice cream and autoerotic asphyxiation.

"Okay, okay. Point taken. So I could stand to lose a few pounds."

"I don't know whether you're trying to bathe me or drown me, but either way you're doing a half-ass job."

"I can't even look at you, 'cause it reminds me how stupid I look."

"God, I love St. Patty's Day! I'm gonna lick green puke until I see double."

Once the cats exhausted their usual conversation topics—that night's costumes, the futility of escape, ringworm—Mr. Whiskers casually introduced the idea of a suicide pact.

"The yarmulke's cute, but was the circumcision really necessary?"

"Never find your owner on Craigs List."

"I love my present! I've always wanted a big shiny indoor tree to tinkle on."

"Maybe licking up that bong water wasn't the smartest idea."

"So where is this 'Swan Lake,' and is it deep enough to drown in?"

"You idiot. You've got me a dressed as a Charlotte when everyone knows I'm a total Carrie."

"Now all I need is a light, a blindfold, and a firing squad."

"If the boys back in the pound could see us now."

"Nothing like spring bloom to remind me how dead I feel inside."

"The cat's laughing his ass off right now."

"Maybe we'll get lucky and he'll carve us up instead."

"I may be drunk, but you're the one who never pets me anymore!"

"How about tightening this tie a little more? Make that a *lot* more."

"One!? I'm only *one*!? Oh for fuck's sake."

"I've had worse things in my mouth.
Yeah, I'm looking at you, Fred."

"You *said*, 'Fetch me my slippers.'"

"Am I freaking you out? Good."

"You want to slap this stupid little hat right off my head, don't you? The feeling's mutual."

"I'm sorry I ate your groceries. How long am I gonna have to wear this?"

"You heard me. I'll get neutered all right . . . in hell!"

"What the—? I can feel you tinkling!"

"Let's see how cute they think I look after I smother their first-born."

"Guess who found your secret stash, mon?"

"Thanks for the birthday sweater. You know what I'd like next year? My fur back!"

"Does this owner make me look fat?"

"Honk if you hate wearing little holiday sweaters in the middle of summer."

"Every year with this shit. Can't they spring for some garden gnomes!"

"What the— I said "I *don't*!"

Subtlety was not the Cat Whisperer's strong suit.

"I liked it better when she punished me by rubbing my face in poop."

"Squeeze a little higher and a hell of a
lot tighter, honey."

"If you need me I'll be milking the cat."

"Why don't you spend a little less time changing my outfits and a lot more time changing my litter box."

"The bad news is I ate the ring. The good news is I've been pooping under your bed."

"I could have sworn I smelled bacon in here."

"Who the fuck is that supposed to be?
Don't quit your day job, Picasso."

"My birthday wish? For you to get a fucking life."

"I can't wait to ride it. Where's the nearest busy intersection?"

"Are you sure you don't want to forget me in the car with the windows rolled up?"

"I like it, but I don't *love* it."

"I'm small now, but my owners say one day I'll grow up to be delicious."

"I'm just like Garfield, except instead of Mondays, I hate all humanity."

Am I dead yet? Please say yes."

"Where the hell's 'thou shalt not dress your dog for cheesy religious cards'?"

"Never thought I'd say this, but I wish I was home licking peanut butter off his balls right now."

"Montezuma, take me now."

"This better be a conjugal visit, sweetheart."

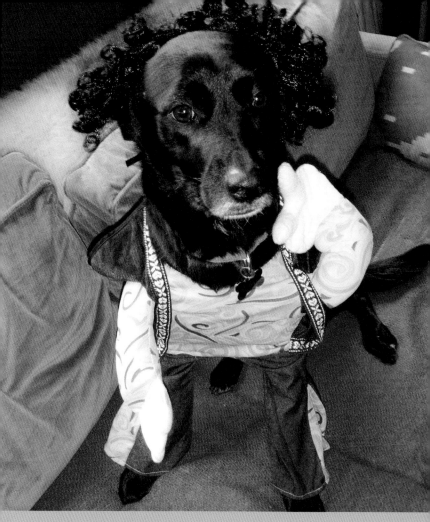

"Put on some Jefferson Airplane and call the cat. It's orgy time."

"Cockadoodle-die."

"Is this my last supper? God, I hope so."

"If his girlfriend makes him dress like that, I guess we don't have much right to complain."

"Your grandpa and grandma didn't even sniff butts until their wedding night."

"Here's the plan. You act cute and distract them while I go dry-hump the ham."

"Just what I wanted for Christmas—a giant rat in a little coat."

"Have you ever considered Internet dating?"

"You know what they say: Don't drink the toilet water in Mexico."

"It's so obvious! What the hell do you mean you don't get my costume?"

"I am sooo gonna hit that."

Toby had the distinct feeling their owner was playing favorites.

Playing fetch, terrorizing the cat, humping the ottoman . . . lately Max wondered what the point of it all was.

"I'm halfway through this crazy thing—where are all the sex positions?"

"Was you not bathing me all month part of this costume?"

"I don't care if you're my master and we're under the mistletoe!"

"Isn't this outfit supposed to come with a poison apple?"

"Okay, Jedi . . . you *really* need a girlfriend."

"How the hell am I supposed to catch fatal pneumonia with this thing on?"

You know it's been a fun Phish show when your dog is the soberest one to drive home.

"How long before he figures out we're stuck?"

"Originally he wanted to fit 'Barack Hussein' on here, too."

First came the obsession with French Existentialism, and now the all-black wardrobe; his owners were beginning to think Willy was depressed.

"How am I supposed to go to the bathroom in this stupid outfi—? Oooww, never mind."

"They say we rockers die too young. I can only hope."

"Remember that time you said you'd rather die than turn 30 single? Take me with you."

"Yeah, I was in the shit. And I'm still in it—I'm just too lazy to move my butt."

"This party's shaved at least eight lives off of me."

"Take the damn picture! I can't keep my gut sucked in forever."

The Reverend stepped in to save the wedding when Bootsy got cold paws.

"Irish I were dead."

"Um . . . why are *you* wearing a tux?"

"Dracula? You're never gonna let me live down that little biting incident, are you?"

"Oh God, what did I do in a past life to deserve this? . . . Oh right, I was Hitler."

"How's me dressing for the gym gonna fix your cottage cheese thighs?"

"If I just stand here long enough, maybe someone will run me over."

The holidays were a particularly contentious time for Emma and Saul.

"I know it's hard to tell if a hound dog's happy or sad, but take a wild guess."

"I hope you like coal in your stocking . . . wet, stinky coal."

"Oh, I get it. I'm just not *exotic* enough for you, is that it?"

"I know I said I'd do a love scene. But nobody told me it would be with a Great Dane!"

"Hey, it's called 'the poop deck' for a reason."

"Okay, where's the hydrant? . . . No,
for me to take a pee."

"That is one lucky turkey."

"I don't remember the movie. If I click my red heels three times will a house fall on me?"

"You want me to *tinkle* the ivories? Okay, whatever you say."

"This isn't half as bad as when she changes my diaper."

"A college degree in this economy? I may as well slit my wrists with this mortarboard."

"Don't look up. Don't look up. Don't look up."

"If I die of embarrassment, please don't bury me like this."

"For the last time, Bill, I'm not Sheila, I don't want to be Sheila, and I never will be Sheila. . . . Although whatever you're cooking us for dinner does smell good."

"I wanna go for a walk . . . off the plank."

"In some countries, I'd be dinner.
Here I eat organic and have my own
Twitter account. God bless America!"